D0056009

Shakespeare's Flowers

Shakespeare's Flowers

CHRONICLE BOOKS
SAN FRANCISCO

First published in the United States by Chronicle Books.

Copyright © 1994 by Pavilion Books, Ltd.

All rights reserved. No part of this book may be reproduced
without written permission from the Publisher.

Printed in China

Library of Congress Cataloging-in-Publication Data available.

ISBN: 0-8118-0836-X

Distributed in Canada by Raincoast Books,
8680 Cambie Street, Vancouver, B.C. V6P 6M9

10 9 8 7 6 5 4 3 2 I

Chronicle Books
275 Fifth St.
San Francisco, CA 94103

CONTENTS

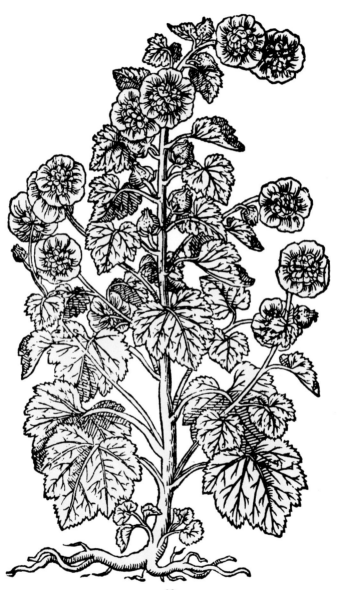

JNTRODUCTION

S HAKESPEARE's expert knowledge on a variety of sub-
jects and professions ranges effortlessly from science to
art, so it comes as no surprise to us that his sublime
words also include imagery of one of the growing fashions of
Tudor times, gardening. His observations of plants and the
beauties of nature stem, however, from his life as a country-
man, not as a botanist. He was able to communicate the
simple pleasures of the scent or colours of flowers in a few
well-chosen words, bringing the plants to life in a fresh and
evocative manner.

Shakespeare speaks lovingly of flowers – in expressions
that are not merely poetical, but faithfully describing what
he daily observed – with obvious affection: 'fresh and fra-
grant flowers', 'the beauteous flowers', 'the sweet summer
buds', 'blossoms passing fair', 'the darling buds of May'.

The herbs, flowers and trees he describes, even when set
in fictitious countries such as 'Illyria', are all English plants
which, with few exceptions, might be seen in the hedgerows
or woods of Warwickshire, in his own or his friends' gardens.
The descriptions are vivid and tell of the countryside he
loved. He introduces many common flowers into his poems
and plays, but there are also some notable omissions, such as
snowdrop, forget-me-not, foxglove, lily-of-the-valley. Yet
violets are mentioned eighteen times, roses over a hundred.

In *A Midsummer Night's Dream* the pansy is the:

> *little western flower,–*
> *Before, milk-white, now purple with love's wound –*
> *And maidens call it love-in-idleness*

which is upon 'sleeping eyelids laid' to weave the magic spell, so central to the plot.

Wild flowers are gathered from their natural habitats – 'flat meads', 'turfy mountains', 'rose-banks', 'unshrubbed down' – but Shakespeare is equally at home in formal gardens with 'pleached bowers' and 'leafy orchards'. Much contemporary folklore, plantlore and herbal knowledge is contained in his colourful language, and also a familiarity with medical 'quackery' in the detailed description of an apothecary's shop in *Romeo and Juliet*.

Yet Shakespeare was neither a peasant nor a village lad, but from good middle-class stock, his father being one of the wealthier citizens of Stratford-upon-Avon. It is not known when he first appeared in London, although the story goes that he had to leave Stratford when caught poaching deer at nearby Charlecote Park. Records show that he became a successful dramatist sometime before 1592, and by 1594 he was a member of the Lord Chamberlain's company, which became the King's Company (of players) in 1603, writing many popular plays for them. He prospered and invested in property at Stratford, where he died in 1616.

In his plays he describes England as a 'sea-walled garden', and some twenty-nine scenes are set in gardens, where characters seek a moment's privacy – or conspiracy – to talk in private, or walk hand-in-hand. In the history plays discussions of national import are often set in gardens – notably with reference to the red and white roses of the houses of York and Lancaster, so fiercely fought over during the fifteenth century in the Wars of the Roses. The white rose was the emblem of the Plantagenet kings, the red of the

Tudors who replaced them, after fearsome battles and considerable treachery.

However, the strong rule of the Tudors ushered in a period of peace and prosperity for the Elizabethans, who were keen gardeners. Medieval garden enclosures expanded into stately 'pleasaunces', with 'curious knotted gardens', pleached alleys, bowling-greens, orchards, vineyards, summer bowers, fountains, dovecotes and beds planted in mixed colours.

Gardens as Shakespeare would have known them were uniform and formal, in every minute detail. Bacon's rule was that a 'garden is best to be square'. The garden was considered to be a continuation of the house, designed to harmonize with the architecture of the building. The square enclosure was bounded either by a high wall or hedge, preferably of hornbeam. Within this space the garden was laid out in formal shapes, with paths and alleys, lined with trees, dividing the square into four or more compartments. All of this was secondary to the great feature of Elizabethan gardens, the knot garden, formed of low hedges of rosemary, dwarf box, thrift or lavender. Sometimes these patterns were in the shape of heraldic beasts, although most surviving designs are abstract and geometric. Sometimes the pattern worked in living green was filled with coloured gravels, sometimes with flowering plants. Other areas of the garden had their own specific purposes: orchards for fruit, kitchen gardens for vegetables, separate gardens for herbs and salading. Salads were very popular, and flowers as well as herbs were often added as edible decoration. Thomas Tusser's book *Five Hundred Points of Good Husbandry*, first published in 1573, went through twelve editions during Elizabeth's reign: testimony to increased interest in gardens among ordinary people.

In 1548 William Turner, the founding father of English botany, published his *New Herball*. Exchanges of knowledge and plants from the Low Countries and Italy were now increasingly influential. Shakespeare was a near contemporary of John Gerard, gardener to Lord Burleigh, who lived from 1545 to 1612. Conjecture has been made that they were acquainted, and that Shakespeare may have seen Gerard's garden, where more than a thousand plants were grown, 'all manner of strange trees, herbes, rootes, plants, flowers and other such rare things'. Gerard published his own famous *Herball* in 1597, partly assembled from the writings of the Flemish botanist Rembert Dodoens, partly from his own observations, with 1,800 woodcut illustrations taken from German woodblocks. It remains a fascinating catalogue of Elizabethan plants and their 'vertues'.

The Elizabethan age, reflected in portraiture and decoration, as well as in verse and literature, shows a strong interest in flowers. Paintings often depict the subject with a flower in the hand, or tucked into a dress, or surrounded by roses. Plasterwork and emblems in books and needlework all represent flowers. Horticultural skills increased, improving flower colouring, increasing their size, or creating double flowers, with acknowledgement to the progress made by the Dutch.

INTRODUCTION

The great houses – Hardwick, Longleat, Theobalds (where Gerard worked) – reflect the glory of this age.

The illustrations for this anthology have been chosen from a pattern book, perhaps for painted cloth or embroidery, dating from the early Tudor period. It is of uncertain origin, but probably East Anglian, being very similar to a rare contemporary manuscript from Helmingham Hall in Suffolk, known as the *Helmingham Herbal* (now in the Mellon Collection). Both give a remarkable picture of natural history in early Tudor times, together with domestic details.

Shakespeare was not only a keen observer of plants, but was also knowledgeable about the more practical side of gardening, often using this knowledge to ironical or dramatic effect, as illustrated by this allegorical extract from *Richard II*:

> *O, what pity is it,*
> *That he had not so trimm'd and dress'd this land*
> *As we this garden! We at time of year*
> *Do wound the bark, the skin of our fruit-trees,*
> *Lest, being over-proud in sap and blood,*
> *With too much riches it confound itself:*
> *Had he done so to great and growing men,*
> *They might have lived to bear and he to taste*
> *Their fruits of duty; superfluous branches*
> *We lop away, that bearing boughs may live:*
> *Had he done so, himself had borne the crown*
> *Which waste of idle hours hath quite thrown down.*

16

⊕HE FLOWERS

KING HENRY VIII

ACT V   SCENE V

Cranmer:

⊤his royal infant, (Heaven still move about her!)
Though in her cradle, yet now promises
Upon this land a thousand thousand blessings,
Which time shall bring to ripeness . . .

She shall be loved, and fear'd: her own shall bless her:
Her foes shake like a field of beaten corn,
And hang their heads with sorrow: good grows with
    her:
In her days every man shall eat in safety,
Under his own vine, what he plants; and sing
The merry songs of peace to all his neighbours:
God shall be truly known; and those about her
From her shall read the perfect ways of honour,
And by those claim their greatness, not by blood . . .

She shall be, to the happiness of England,
An agèd princess; many days shall see her,
And yet no day without a deed to crown it.
Would I had known no more! but she must die –
She must, the saints must have her – yet a virgin;
A most unspotted lily shall she pass
To the ground, and all the world shall mourn her.

17

THE ASPHODEL

A WINTER'S TALE

ACT IV   SCENE III

Perdita:

Now, my fairest friend,
I would I had some flowers o' the spring, that might
Become your time of day; and yours, and yours;
That wear upon your virgin branches yet
Your maidenheads growing: – O, Proserpina,
For the flowers now, that, frighted, thou lett'st fall
From Dis's waggon! daffodils,
That come before the swallow dares, and take
The winds of March with beauty; violets, dim,
But sweeter than the lids of Juno's eyes,
Or Cytherea's breath; pale primroses,
That die unmarried, ere they can behold
Bright Phœbus in his strength, a malady
Most incident to maids; bold oxlips, and
The crown-imperial; lilies of all kinds,
The flower-de-luce being one! Oh! these I lack,
To make you garlands of; and, my sweet friend,
To strew him o'er and o'er.

THE DAISY

LOVE'S LABOUR'S LOST

ACT V   SCENE II

SONG

SPRING

I

When daisies pied, and violets blue,
    And lady-smocks all silver white,
And cuckoo-buds of yellow hue,
    Do paint the meadows with delight,
The cuckoo then, on every tree,
Mocks married men, for thus sings he,
                Cuckoo;
Cuckoo, cuckoo, – O word of fear,
Unpleasing to a married ear!

II

When shepherds pipe on oaten straws,
    And merry larks are ploughmen's clocks,
When turtles tread, and rooks, and daws,
    And maidens bleach their summer smocks,
The cuckoo then, on every tree,
Mocks married men, for thus sings he,
                Cuckoo;
Cuckoo, cuckoo, – O word of fear,
Unpleasing to a married ear!

ᲧHE STRAWBERRY

KING HENRY V

ACT I   SCENE V

Ely:

The strawberry grows underneath the nettle;
And wholesome berries thrive and ripen best
Neighbour'd by fruit of baser quality:
And so the prince obscured his contemplation
Under the veil of wildness; which, no doubt,
Grew like the summer grass, fastest by night,
Unseen, yet crescive in his faculty.

Canterbury:

It must be so; for miracles are ceased;
And therefore we must needs admit the means
How things are perfected.

BROOM

THE TEMPEST

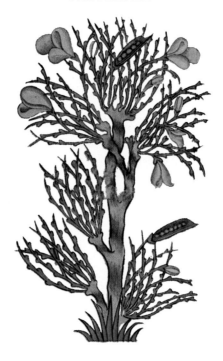

ACT I   SCENE I

Gonzalo:

Now would I give a thousand furlongs of sea for an acre of barren ground; ling, heath, broom, furze, anything. The wills above be done! but I would fain die a dry death.

THE POPPY

ACT III   SCENE III

Iago:

I will in Cassio's lodging lose this napkin,
And let him find it. Trifles, light as air,
Are to the jealous confirmations strong
As proofs of holy writ. This may do something.
The Moor already changes with my poison:
Dangerous conceits are, in their natures, poisons,
Which, at the first, are scarce found to distaste;
But, with a little act upon the blood,
Burn like the mines of sulphur. – I did say so –
Look, where he comes! Not poppy, nor mandragora,
Nor all the drowsy syrups of the world,
Shall ever medicine thee to that sweet sleep
Which thou ow'dst yesterday.

THE TEMPEST

ACT V   SCENE I

Ariel:

Where the bee sucks, there suck I;
In a cowslip's bell I lie:
There I couch when owls do cry.
On the bat's back I do fly
After summer merrily.
Merrily, merrily, shall I live now,
Under the blossom that hangs on the bough.

24

THE COWSLIP

ACT II   SCENE I

Puck:

How now, spirit! whither wander you?

Fairy:

Over hill, over dale,
  Thorough bush, thorough briar,
Over park, over pale,
  Thorough flood, thorough fire,
I do wander everywhere,
Swifter than the moon's sphere;
And I serve the fairy queen,
To dew her orbs upon the green:
The cowslips tall her pensioners be;
In their gold coats spots you see;
Those be rubies, fairy favours,
In those freckles live their savours:
I must go seek some dew-drops here,
And hang a pearl in every cowslip's ear.
Farewell, thou lob of spirits, I'll be gone;
Our queen and all her elves come here anon.

CAMOMILE

KING HENRY IV, PART I

ACT II   SCENE IV

Falstaff:

Peace, good pint-pot; peace, good tickle-brain. – Harry, I do not only marvel where thou spendest thy time, but also how thou art accompanied: for though the camomile, the more it is trodden the faster it grows, yet youth, the more it is wasted the sooner it wears.

THE COLUMBINE

THE DAISY

HAMLET

ACT IV   SCENE VII

Queen:

There is a willow grows aslant a brook,
That shows his hoar leaves in the glassy stream;
There, with fantastic garlands did she come,
Of crow-flowers, nettles, daisies, and long purples,
That liberal shepherds give a grosser name,
But our cold maids do dead men's fingers call them:
There, on the pendent boughs her coronet weeds
Clambering to hang, an envious sliver broke;
When down the weedy trophies, and herself,
Fell in the weeping brook. Her clothes spread wide;
And, mermaid-like, a while they bore her up:
Which time, she chanted snatches of old tunes;
As one incapable of her own distress,
Or like a creature native and indued
Unto that element: but long it could not be,
Till that her garments, heavy with their drink,
Pull'd the poor wretch from her melodious lay
To muddy death.

THE EGLANTINE

A MIDSUMMER NIGHT'S DREAM

ACT II   SCENE I

Oberon:

I know a bank where the wild thyme blows,
Where ox-lips and the nodding violet grows;
Quite over-canopied with luscious woodbine,
With sweet musk-roses, and with eglantine:
There sleeps Titania, sometime of the night,
Lull'd in these flowers with dances and delight;
And there the snake throws her enamell'd skin,
Weed wide enough to wrap a fairy in:
And with the juice of this I'll streak her eyes,
And make her full of hateful fantasies.
Take thou some of it, and seek through this grove:
A sweet Athenian lady is in love
With a disdainful youth: anoint his eyes;
But do it when the next thing he espies
May be the lady. Thou shalt know the man
By the Athenian garments he hath on.
Effect it with some care; that he may prove
More fond on her, than she upon her love:
And look thou meet me ere the first cock crow.

VETCH

THE TEMPEST

ACT IV   SCENE I

Iris:

Ceres, most bounteous lady, thy rich leas
Of wheat, rye, barley, vetches, oats, and pease;
Thy turfy mountains, where live nibbling sheep,
And flat meads thatch'd with stover, them to keep;
Thy banks with pioned and twilled brims,
Which spongy April at thy hest betrims,
To make cold nymphs chaste crowns; and thy broom
    groves,
Whose shadow the dismissed bachelor loves,
Being lass-lorn; thy pole-clipp'd vineyard;
And thy sea-marge steril, and rocky hard,
Where thou thyself dost air: the queen o' the sky,
Whose watery arch, and messenger, am I,
Bids thee leave these; and with her sovereign grace,
Here on this grass-plot, in this very place,
To come and sport: her peacocks fly amain:
Approach, rich Ceres, her to entertain.

THE VINE

ACT IV   SCENE I

Ceres:

Earth's increase, foison plenty,
Barns and garners never empty;
Vines with clustering bunches growing;
Plants with goodly burden bowing:
Spring come to you, at the farthest,
In the very end of harvest!
Scarcity and want shall shun you;
Ceres' blessing so is on you.

THE MARIGOLD

Let those who are in favour with their stars,
Of public honour and proud titles boast,
Whilst I, whom fortune of such triumph bars,
Unlook'd for joy in that I honour most.
Great princes' favourites their fair leaves spread
But as the marigold at the sun's eye;
And in themselves their pride lies burièd,
For at a frown they in their glory die.
The painful warrior famoused for fight,
After a thousand victories once foil'd,
Is from the book of honour razèd quite,
And all the rest forgot for which he toil'd:
   Then happy I, that love and am beloved
   Where I may not remove, nor be removed.

THE RAPE OF LUCRECE

Her lily hand her rosy cheek lies under,
Cozening the pillow of a lawful kiss;
Who, therefore angry, seems to part in sunder,
Swelling on either side to want his bliss;
Between whose hills her head entombed is:
   Where, like a virtuous monument, she lies,
   To be admired of lewd unhallow'd eyes.

Without the bed her other fair hand was,
On the green coverlet; whose perfect white
Show'd like an April daisy on the grass,
With pearly sweat, resembling dew of night.
Her eyes, like marigolds, had sheathed their light,
   And canopied in darkness sweetly lay,
   Till they might open to adorn the day.

Her hair, like golden threads, play'd with her
      breath;
O modest wantons! wanton modesty!
Showing life's triumph in the map of death,
And death's dim look in life's mortality:
Each in her sleep themselves so beautify,
   As if between them twain there were no strife,
   But that life lived in death, and death in life.

THE DAFFODIL

ACT IV   SCENE II

Autolycus:

When daffodils begin to peer,
  With heigh! the doxy over the dale,
Why then comes in the sweet o' the year;
  For the red blood reigns in the winter's pale.

The white sheet bleaching on the hedge,
  With heigh! the sweet birds, O, how they sing!
Doth set my pugging tooth on edge;
  For a quart of ale is a dish for a king.

The lark that tirra-lirra chants,
  With heigh! with heigh! the thrush and the jay:
Are summer songs for me and my aunts,
  While we lie tumbling in the hay.

THE CARNATION

ACT IV   SCENE III

Perdita:

For you there's rosemary, and rue; these keep
Seeming, and savour, all the winter long:
Grace, and remembrance, be to you both,
And welcome to our shearing!

Polixenes:

Shepherdess,
(A fair one are you,) well you fit our ages
With flowers of winter.

Perdita:

Sir, the year growing ancient, –
Not yet on summer's death, nor on the birth
Of trembling winter, – the fairest flowers o' the season
Are our carnations, and streak'd gillyvors,
Which some call nature's bastards: of that kind
Our rustic garden's barren; and I care not
To get slips of them.

37

HYSSOP

OTHELLO

ACT I   SCENE III

Iago:

Virtue? a fig! 'tis in ourselves that we are thus, or thus. Our bodies are our gardens; to the which our wills are gardeners: so that if we will plant nettles, or sow lettuce; set hyssop, and weed up thyme; supply it with one gender of herbs, or distract it with many; either to have it sterile with idleness, or manured with industry; why, the power and corrigible authority of this lies in our wills. If the balance of our lives had not one scale of reason to poise another of sensuality, the blood and baseness of our natures would conduct us to most preposterous conclusions: but we have reason to cool our raging motions, our carnal stings, our unbitted lusts; whereof I take this, that you call love, to be a sect or scion.

Rosemary

ROMEO AND JULIET

ACT IV   SCENE V

Friar Laurence:

Peace, ho, for shame! confusion's cure lives not
In these confusions. Heaven and yourself
Had part in this fair maid; now Heaven hath all,
And all the better is it for the maid:
Your part in her you could not keep from death;
But Heaven keeps his part in eternal life.
The most you sought was – her promotion;
For 'twas your heaven, she should be advanced:
And weep ye now, seeing she is advanced,
Above the clouds, as high as heaven itself?
O, in this love, you love your child so ill,
That you run mad, seeing that she is well:
She's not well married that lives married long;
But she's best married that dies married young.
Dry up your tears, and stick your rosemary
On this fair corse; and, as the custom is,
In all her best array bear her to church:
For though some nature bids us all lament,
Yet nature's tears are reason's merriment.

HE LILY

THE PASSIONATE PILGRIM

Fair is my love, but not so fair as fickle;
Mild as a dove, but neither true nor trusty;
Brighter than glass, and yet, as glass is, brittle;
Softer than wax, and yet, as iron, rusty:
   A lily pale, with damask dye to grace her,
   None fairer, nor none falser to deface her.

Her lips to mine how often hath she join'd,
Between each kiss her oaths of true love swearing!
How many tales to please me hath she coin'd,
Dreading my love, the loss thereof still fearing!
   Yet in the midst of all her pure protestings,
   Her faith, her oaths, her tears, and all were jestings.

She burn'd with love, as straw with fire flameth,
She burn'd out love, as soon as straw outburneth,
She framed the love, and yet she foil'd the framing,
She bade love last, and yet she fell a-turning.
   Was this a lover, or a lecher whether?
   Bad in the best, though excellent in neither.

41

ℬELLADONNA

ROMEO AND JULIET

ACT II   SCENE III

Friar Laurence:

The gray-eyed morn smiles on the frowning night,
Checkering the eastern clouds with streaks of light;
And flecked darkness like a drunkard reels
From forth day's path, and Titan's fiery wheels:
Now ere the sun advance his burning eye,
The day to cheer, and night's dank dew to dry,
I must up-fill this osier cage of ours,
With baleful weeds, and precious-juicèd flowers.
The earth, that's nature's mother, is her tomb;
What is her burying grave, that is her womb:
And from her womb children of divers kind
We sucking on her natural bosom find;
Many for many virtues excellent,
None but for some, and yet all different.
O, mickle is the powerful grace, that lies
In plants, herbs, stones, and their true qualities:
For nought so vile that on the earth doth live,
But to the earth some special good doth give;
Nor aught so good, but, strain'd from that fair use,

Revolts from true birth, stumbling on abuse:
Virtue itself turns vice, being misapplied;
And vice sometime's by action dignified.
Within the infant rind of this weak flower
Poison hath residence, and medicine power:
For this, being smelt, with that part cheers each part;
Being tasted, slays all senses with the heart.
Two such opposèd kings encamp them still
In man as well as herbs, – grace, and rude will;
And, where the worser is predominant,
Full soon the canker death eats up that plant.

THE VIOLET

TWELFTH NIGHT; OR, WHAT YOU WILL

ACT I   SCENE I

Orsino, Duke of Illyria:

If music be the food of love, play on;
Give me excess of it; that, surfeiting,
The appetite may sicken, and so die. –
That strain again! – it had a dying fall:
Oh, it came o'er my ear like the sweet sound
That breathes upon a bank of violets,
Stealing and giving odour! – Enough; no more;
'Tis not so sweet now, as it was before.
O spirit of love, how quick and fresh art thou!
That notwithstanding thy capacity
Receiveth as the sea, nought enters there,
Of what validity and pitch soever,
But falls into abatement and low price,
Even in a minute! so full of shapes is fancy,
That it alone is high-fantastical.

PERICLES

ACT IV   SCENE I

Marina:

No: I will rob Tellus of her weed,
To strew thy green with flowers: the yellows, blues,
The purple violets, and marigolds,
Shall as a carpet hang upon thy grave,
While summer days do last. Ah me! poor maid,
Born in a tempest, when my mother died,
This world to me is like a lasting storm,
Whirring me from my friends.

THE VIOLET

The forward violet thus did I chide:
  Sweet thief, whence didst thou steal thy sweet that
     smells,
If not from my love's breath? The purple pride
Which on thy soft cheek for complexion dwells
In my love's veins thou hast too grossly dyed.
The lily I condemned for thy hand,
And buds of marjoram had stol'n thy hair;
The roses fearfully on thorns did stand,
One blushing shame, another white despair;
A third, nor red nor white, had stol'n of both,
And to his robbery had annex'd thy breath;
But, for his theft, in pride of all his growth
A vengeful canker eat him up to death.
  More flowers I noted, yet I none could see
  But sweet or colour it had stol'n from thee.

MINT

A WINTER'S TALE

ACT IV   SCENE III

Perdita:

Here's flowers for you;
Hot lavender, mints, savory, marjoram;
The marigold, that goes to bed with the sun,
And with him rises weeping; these are flowers
Of middle summer, and, I think, they are given
To men of middle age: you are very welcome.

RUSHES

ACT III   SCENE I

Owen Glendower:

She bids you on the wanton rushes lay you down,
And rest your gentle head upon her lap,
And she will sing the song that pleaseth you,
And on your eyelids crown the god of sleep,
Charming your blood with pleasing heaviness;
Making such difference betwixt wake and sleep,
As is the difference betwixt day and night,
The hour before the heavenly-harness'd team
Begins his golden progress in the east.

Mortimer:

With all my heart I'll sit and hear her sing:
By that time will our book, I think, be drawn.

Glendower:

Do so;
And those musicians that shall play to you,
Hang in the air a thousand leagues from hence;
And straight they shall be here: sit, and attend.

ARLIC

A MIDSUMMER NIGHT'S DREAM

ACT IV   SCENE II

Bottom:

Not a word of me. All that I will tell you is, that the duke hath dined: – get your apparel together; good strings to your beards, new ribbons to your pumps; meet presently at the palace; every man look o'er his part; for, the short and the long is, our play is preferred. In any case, let Thisby have clean linen: and let not him that plays the lion pare his nails, for they shall hang out for the lion's claws. And, most dear actors, eat no onions, nor garlic, for we are to utter sweet breath; and I do not doubt but to hear them say it is a sweet comedy. No more words; away; go, away.

THE PANSY

ACT II   SCENE I

Oberon:

That very time I saw, (but thou couldst not,)
Flying between the cold moon and the earth,
Cupid all arm'd: a certain aim he took
At a fair vestal, thronèd by the west;
And loosed his love-shaft smartly from his bow,
As it should pierce a hundred thousand hearts:
But I might see young Cupid's fiery shaft
Quench'd in the chaste beams of the watery moon;
And the imperial votaress passed on,
In maiden meditation, fancy-free.
Yet mark'd I where the bolt of Cupid fell:
It fell upon a little western flower, –
Before, milk-white, now purple with love's wound –
And maidens call it love-in-idleness.
Fetch me that flower: the herb I show'd thee once;
The juice of it on sleeping eyelids laid,
Will make or man or woman madly dote
Upon the next live creature that it sees.
Fetch me this herb: and be thou here again,
Ere the leviathan can swim a league.

50

Puck:

I'll put a girdle round about the earth
In forty minutes.

Oberon:

Having once this juice,
I'll watch Titania when she is asleep,
And drop the liquor of it in her eyes:
The next thing then she waking looks upon,
(Be it on lion, bear, or wolf, or bull,
On meddling monkey, or on busy ape,)
She shall pursue it with the soul of love.
And ere I take this charm off from her sight,
(As I can take it, with another herb,)
I'll make her render up her page to me.
But who comes here? I am invisible;
And I will overhear their conference.

ACT III   SCENE II

Oberon:

Then crush this herb into Lysander's eye,
Whose liquor hath this virtuous property,
To take from thence all error, with his might,
And make his eyeballs roll with wonted sight.
When they next wake, all this derision
Shall seem a dream, and fruitless vision;
And back to Athens shall the lovers wend,
With league, whose date till death shall never end.
Whiles I in this affair do thee employ,
I'll to my queen, and beg her Indian boy;
And then I will her charmed eye release
From monster's view, and all things shall be peace.

THE ROSE

SONNET LIV

O how much more doth beauty beauteous seem,
By that sweet ornament which truth doth give!
The rose looks fair, but fairer we it deem
For that sweet odour which doth in it live.
The canker-blooms have full as deep a dye
As the perfumèd tincture of the roses,
Hang on such thorns, and play as wantonly
When summer's breath their masked buds discloses;
But, for their virtue only is their show,
They live unwoo'd, and unrespected fade;
Die to themselves. Sweet roses do not so;
Of their sweet deaths are sweetest odours made:
   And so of you, beauteous and lovely youth,
   When that shall fade, by verse distils your truth.

THE FOXGLOVE

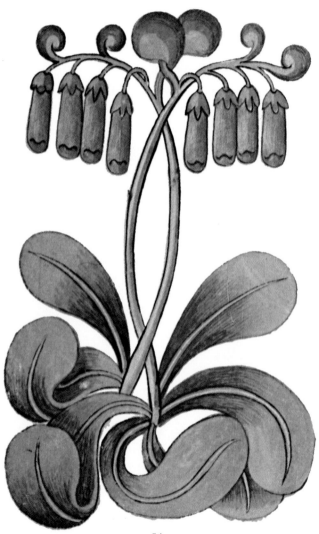

THE BLACKBERRY

AS YOU LIKE IT

ACT III   SCENE II

Rosalind:

No; I will not cast away my physic but on those that are sick. There is a man haunts the forest that abuses our young plants with carving *Rosalind* on their barks; hangs odes upon hawthorns, and elegies on brambles; all, forsooth, deifying the name of Rosalind: if I could meet that fancy-monger I would give him some good counsel, for he seems to have the quotidian of love upon him.

Orlando:

I am he that is so love-shaked; I pray you, tell me your remedy.

Rosalind:

There is none of my uncle's marks upon you: he taught me how to know a man in love; in which cage of rushes, I am sure, you are not prisoner.

THE OAK

A MIDSUMMER NIGHT'S DREAM

ACT II   SCENE I

Puck:

The king doth keep his revels here tonight;
Take heed, the queen come not within his sight,
For Oberon is passing fell and wrath,
Because that she, as her attendant, hath
A lovely boy stolen from an Indian king;
She never had so sweet a changeling:
And jealous Oberon would have the child
Knight of his train, to trace the forests wild:
But she, perforce, withholds the lovèd boy
Crowns him with flowers, and makes him all her joy:
And now they never meet in grove, or green,
By fountain clear, or spangled starlight sheen,
But they do square; that all their elves, for fear,
Creep into acorn-cups, and hide them there.

ℛUE

HAMLET

ACT IV   SCENE V

Ophelia:

There's rosemary, that's for remembrance; *pray, love, remember*: and there is pansies, that's for thoughts.

Laertes:

A document in madness; thoughts and remembrance fitted.

Ophelia:

There's fennel for you, and columbines: – there's rue for you; and here's some for me: – we may call it herb of grace o'Sundays: – oh, you must wear your rue with a difference. – There's a daisy: – I would give you some violets; but they withered all, when my father died: – they say, he made a good end. –

ⒹHE POMEGRANATE

ROMEO AND JULIET

ACT III   SCENE V

Juliet:

Wilt thou be gone? it is not yet near day:
It was the nightingale, and not the lark,
That pierced the fearful hollow of thine ear;
Nightly she sings on yon pomegranate-tree:
Believe me, love, it was the nightingale.

Romeo:

It was the lark, the herald of the morn,
No nightingale: look, love, what envious streaks
Do lace the severing clouds in yonder east:
Night's candles are burnt out, and jocund day
Stands tiptoe on the misty mountain tops;
I must be gone and live, or stay and die.

Juliet:

Yon light is not daylight, I know it, I:
It is some meteor that the sun exhales,
To be to thee this night a torch-bearer,
And light thee on thy way to Mantua:
Therefore stay yet, thou need'st not to be gone.

58

THE MULBERRY

ACT III   SCENE I

Titania:

Be kind and courteous to this gentleman;
Hop in his walks, and gambol in his eyes;
Feed him with apricocks, and dewberries;
With purple grapes, green figs, and mulberries;
The honey-bags steal from the humble-bees,
And, for night-tapers, crop their waxen thighs,
And light them at the fiery glow-worm's eyes,
To have my love to bed, and to arise;
And pluck the wings from painted butterflies,
To fan the moonbeams from his sleeping eyes:
Nod to him, elves, and do him courtesies.

THE CHERRY

ACT III   SCENE II

Helena:

We, Hermia, like two artificial gods,
Have with our needles created both one flower,
Both on one sampler, sitting on one cushion,
Both warbling of one song, both in one key;
As if our hands, our sides, voices, and minds,
Had been incorporate. So we grew together,
Like to a double cherry, seeming parted;
But yet a union in partition,
Two lovely berries moulded on one stem:
So, with two seeming bodies, but one heart,
Two of the first, like coats in heraldry,
Due but to one, and crowned with one crest.
And will you rent our ancient love asunder,
To join with men in scorning your poor friend?
It is not friendly, 'tis not maidenly:
Our sex, as well as I, may chide you for it;
Though I alone do feel the injury.

CLOVER

ACT V SCENE II

Duke of Burgundy:

My duty to you both, on equal love,
Great kings of France and England! That I have
    labour'd
With all my wits, my pains, and strong
    endeavours,
To bring your most imperial majesties
Unto this bar and royal interview,
Your mightiness on both parts best can witness.
Since then my office hath so far prevail'd
That face to face, and royal eye to eye,
You have congreeted; let it not disgrace me,
If I demand, before this royal view,
What rub, or what impediment, there is,
Why that the naked, poor, and mangled peace,
Dear nurse of arts, plenties, and joyful births,
Should not, in this best garden of the world,
Our fertile France, put up her lovely visage?
Alas! she hath from France too long been chased;
And all her husbandry doth lie on heaps,
Corrupting in its own fertility.
Her vine, the merry cheerer of the heart,
Unprunèd dies: her hedges even-pleach'd,
Like prisoners wildly overgrown with hair,
Put forth disorder'd twigs: her fallow leas
The darnel, hemlock, and rank fumitory,
Doth root upon; while that the coulter rusts,
That should deracinate such savagery:
The even mead, that erst brought sweetly forth
The freckled cowslip, burnet, and green clover,

Wanting the scythe, all uncorrected, rank,
Conceives by idleness; and nothing teems
But hateful docks, rough thistles, kecksies, burs,
Losing both beauty and utility:
And as our vineyards, fallows, meads, and
        hedges,
Defective in their natures, grow to wildness,
Even so our houses, and ourselves, and children,
Have lost, or do not learn, for want of time,
The sciences that should become our country;
But grow like savages, – as soldiers will,
That nothing do but meditate on blood, –
To swearing, and stern looks, diffused attire,
And everything that seems unnatural.
Which to reduce into our former favour
You are assembled; and my speech entreats
That I may know the let, why gentle peace
Should not expel these inconveniences,
And bless us with her former qualities.

THE ROSE

My mistress' eyes are nothing like the sun;
Coral is far more red than her lips' red:
If snow be white, why then her breasts are dun;
If hairs be wires, black wires grow on her head.
I have seen roses damask'd, red and white,
But no such roses see I in her cheeks;
And in some perfumes is there more delight
Than in the breath that from my mistress reeks.
I love to hear her speak, – yet well I know
That music hath a far more pleasing sound;
I grant I never saw a goddess go, –
My mistress, when she walks, treads on the
   ground;
   And yet, by heaven, I think my love as rare
   As any she belied with false compare.

THE THISTLE

OUR SEA-WALLED GARDEN

KING RICHARD II

ACT III   SCENE IV

Gardener:

Go, bind thou up yon' dangling apricocks,
Which, like unruly children, make their sire
Stoop with oppression of their prodigal weight:
Give some supportance to the bending twigs.
Go thou, and, like an executioner,
Cut off the heads of too-fast-growing sprays,
That look too lofty in our commonwealth:
All must be even in our government.
You thus employ'd, I will go root away
The noisome weeds, that without profit suck
The soil's fertility from wholesome flowers.

Servant:

Why should we, in the compass of a pale,
Keep law, and form, and due proportion,
Showing, as in a model, our firm estate,
When our sea-walled garden, the whole land,
Is full of weeds; her fairest flowers choked up,
Her fruit-trees all unpruned, her hedges ruin'd,
Her knots disorder'd, and her wholesome herbs
Swarming with caterpillars?

Picture Credits

p.10: Double purple hollihocke from John Gerarde's *Herball*, 1597 (Royal Horticultural Society, Lindley Library, London)
p.11: Gateway to an Elizabethan herb garden from Cats' *Emblems*, 1622
p.13: Title page of Hans Sibmacher's *Neues Modelbuch*, 1604
p.16: Elizabeth I by Nicholas Hilliard (Courtesy of the Board of Trustees of the Victoria & Albert Museum, London)

The flower illustrations are taken from MS Ashmole 1504, reproduced by courtesy of the Bodleian Library, Oxford. Folio numbers, from which the details are taken, are listed after the page numbers: p.5: folio 23; p.6: folio 24v; p.7: folio 10; p.9: folio 3; p.16: folio 12; p.17: folio 6; pp.18, 19: folio 3; pp.20, 21: folio 4; pp.22, 23: folio 5; pp.24, 25: folio 6; p.26: folio 7; p.27: folio 6v; p.28: folio 7v; p.29: folio 7; p.30: folio 3; p.31: folio 8v; p.32: folio 23; p.33: folio 25; pp.34, 35: folio 9; p.36: folio 9v; p.37: folio 10; p.38: folio 11; p.39: folio 16; pp.40, 41: folio 12; p.42: folio 3; p.43: folio 13; pp.44, 45: folio 19; p.46: folio 14; p.47: folio 13v; pp.48, 49: folio 16v; p.50: folio 11; p.52: folio 6; p.53: folio 24v; p.54: folio 15v; p.55: folio 21; p.56: folio 23v; p.57: folio 17; p.58: folio 3; p.59: folio 21v; p.60: folio 22v; p.61: folio 25v; p.63: folio 18; p.64: folio 25; p.65: folio 18v; p.66: folio 6; p.67: folio 20v.